FOR THE *Levites*

A CLOSER WALK WITH JESUS
BEYOND THE MUSIC

Devotional and Prayer Journal
for Ministers of Music

by

Natasha Richards

Watersprings
PUBLISHING

FOR THE LEVITES
Published by Watersprings Publishing, a division of
Watersprings Media House, LLC.
P.O. Box 1284
Olive Branch, MS 38654
www.waterspringsmedia.com
Contact publisher for bulk orders and permission requests.

Printed in the United States of America.

ISBN 13: 978-1-948877-49-7

This book is dedicated to Bonnye Johnson
who I affectionately call "Auntie Bonnye."
I approached her many years ago and asked her
if she could teach me how to sing.
She replied, "No, I am not going to teach you how to sing.
I am going to teach you about your relationship with God
and your ministry. You already know how to sing."

Table of Contents

Acknowledgements

God, You are the Being that has graciously and miraculously devoted Yourself to loving me and I thank You. I thank You for allowing me to be able to use the great and stormy moments of my ministry to write this devotional. I pray that anyone who reads or knows of this book will be blessed. I pray they will have a closer walk with You.

Mom, thank you for teaching me about working hard and sticking to a goal. There are not enough words, or any significant gift I can give to you to properly say thank you.

Dad, thank you for teaching me to know what is real.

Selena, you are my creative gem. Thank you for inspiring me to do what I love, "Mom just try…"

Leilani, you are my great reminder. Thank you for pushing, "Mom you should sing more…."

To my Pillars: The Black Ops Team & Mentors, thank you for being real people of God.

To my Zamar Board: It has been an amazing joy to work with all of you.

Introduction

Music is used in farewells (Genesis 31:27), as entertainment (Isaiah 5:12), for weddings (Jeremiah 7:34), funerals (Matthew 9:18, 23), sacred processions (I Chronicles 13:6-8), victory celebrations (Exodus 15:20, 21), coronation services (2 Chronicles 23:11, 13), and dedication services (2 Chronicles 5:11-13).

Ministers have a duty to preach the gospel (I Corinthians 1:17), to preach Christ crucified (I Corinthians 1:23), to preach Christ's riches (Ephesians 3:8-12), to feed the church (John 21:15-17), to edify the church (Ephesians 4:12), to pray for people (Colossians 1:9), to teach (2 Timothy 2:2), to exhort (Titus 1:9), to rebuke (Titus 2:15), to warn of apostasy (2 Timothy 4:2-5), to comfort (2 Corinthians 1:4-6), and to win souls (I Corinthians 9:19-23). Can music and the spoken word be combined? Yes, they can.

Music forms a part of God's worship in the courts above. We should endeavor in songs of praise, to approach as nearly as possible the harmony of the heavenly choirs. This doesn't happen by chance, but requires training. Therefore, studies in music, music theory, and proper vocal training should not be neglected or taken lightly. Singing, and the offering of music is as much a part of a religious service, and as much an act of worship as prayer. The heart, feeling the spirit of the song adds to the song expression and ushers those in attendance into the presence of God. *"When it comes to Music Ministry, you must remove self and give total praise to God to hopefully win, convert, and touch someone's heart. It is all about soul winning..."* -Elder Earl Mike, Orlando Florida. As Levites we incorporate this thought as we prepare to go beyond the music.

Who are the Levites? Here are some things I have learned:

- Levites were set apart. (Numbers 3:41)
- The Levites' support came from the tithe of other tribes. (Numbers 18:20-25)
- Levites were included in the category of the poor and widowed, those we should take care of. (Deuteronomy 12:19, 14:27-29)
- Levites were officials, judges, gatekeepers and musicians who assisted the priest. (I Chronicles 23:4-5}

(Bullet point taken from Elwell, Walter A. "Entry for Levite." Evangelical Dictionary of Theory 1997" and Baker's Evangelical Dictionary of Biblical Theory-Levite.)

In the many times I have heard the Levites name voiced, it has been associated with worship or music. When I think of the Levites, I think of soldiers all lined up getting ready for battle with the soldiers all standing tall in a uniformed militant stance, waiting for their captain's orders. But then you hear and see a group of people dressed in a priestly manner begin to worship God just because He is God. They begin to open their mouths and raise their hands with boisterous praise. The soldiers and everyone around them begin to feel the Holy Spirit fall on them. In this moment, the soldiers are filled with the confidence of God and they know whether they win or lose, they have won something that day. They know that God is with them. The Levites continue their worship and lead the soldiers into battle by blowing their trumpets. The Levites set the atmosphere for the Holy Spirit to do His work.

The responsibility of a Levite life is deeper than you can ever imagine. As you embark on this journey of prayer, I pray that not only does your music ministry grow stronger, but that you choose to dive deeper into your relationship with God. To be a Levite means we must have an amazing relationship with God. It means taking a journey to die to self and live in Christ daily.[1]

Below is the icon key. Please refer to it as you use this devotional. At the beginning of each devotional there is a scripture from the Bible for you to read. At the end of each devotional there is a thought for you to consider and write about in your journal. Additionally, a starter prayer is provided to guide you into your daily prayer time.

Icon Key

Journal Writing

Prayer Starter

Bible Reading

PART 1

Your Journey

The journey begins with seeking God. Before you take a run/walk you need proper directions, proper nourishment, and proper rest. We are about to travel down a road and along the way we will learn a few things. To endure all we will encounter along the journey, we will learn how to properly arm ourselves and recognize the lessons of our past so we can continue into our future. We will also learn to purify our hearts that God may have a clean home in which to dwell. We will learn all of this so that our lives may be acceptable to God.

1

The Armor of God: How Prepared Are You?

Ephesians 6:12-13 NIV

For our struggle is not against flesh and blood, but against the rulers, against the authorities, against the powers of this dark world and against the spiritual forces of evil in the heavenly realms. Therefore put on the full armor of God, so that when the day of evil comes, you may be able to stand your ground, and after you have done everything, to stand.

We have chosen to be a part of a ministry; the Ministry of Music. A song, written from the heart of God has the potential to be more effective at soul-winning than a sermon. For this reason, we who minister through music, need to arm ourselves with all that is God. We do this not just by reading the Bible, but by comprehending and implementing it into our lives. This perspective converts the songs we sing from mere performance, to the purposeful and powerful act of testifying and telling others about God.[1]

Our song is someone's conduit to salvation; therefore, as those who minister in music we must see that our ministry goes well beyond church services. Consequently, no longer can we play around by doing whatever we want outside of our ministry. We have to consider how our everyday lives affect our ministries. What does this mean? Our focus text teaches us that we deal with spirits and principalities that are not of this world. When we go out and defy GOD it will present itself as chaos in our music ministry. Have you ever been a part of a ministry and at first everything seems to be going well, then all of a sudden the atmosphere in the ministry changes for the worse? Things planned for the ministry do not go well and there is always a battle to get anything done correctly. Many times that stems from the introduction of imbalance. There must be balance! We must not ride the fence! Instead, we must choose God and the tools He has given us to battle, or we may not survive the demands of ministry, let alone our own personal struggles. We have chosen to be a part of a group that the devil does not want to succeed. Understand, at every turn we will be tried. However, if we have a relationship and a love for the true God, whom we have been given the privilege to sing about, He will strengthen us every time.

Pray

Father, I understand the journey of music ministry has many obstacles, but I pray today that I seek all that is You. I pray I will put on the full armor of God, so that when the day of evil comes I will stand my ground. God, let me be one to not only sing Your words, but live them as well.

Write

Becoming a better you is an ongoing quest. What steps can you take to arm yourself in God for the achievement of a better you? Remember we have a journey ahead. Are you strong enough to endure, and can you encourage someone else to do the same?

2

No Past. . .Future

Philippians 3:13-14, NIV

Brothers and sisters, I do not consider myself yet to have taken hold of it. But one thing I do: Forgetting what is behind and straining toward what is ahead, I press on toward the goal to win the prize for which God has called me heavenward in Christ Jesus.

There are times when we tend to allow the past to dictate the decisions we make, but when we become God's very own we need to let Him lead; not our past. Consider this scenario: We've worked very hard in rehearsals to make sure we have the proper sound, but our director constantly keeps reminding us of our past mistakes. What would happen to our morale or energy? The same thing happens when we rehearse our life mistakes. We destroy our motivation to move forward. Instead of bringing our past into today, we must make the decision to let our past stay where it is. The devil has a tendency to encourage us to allow the spirit of discouragement to envelop us, especially when we are trying hard to make correct decisions on our journey. We need to be in a prayerful state at all times, it is our constant communication coupled with our practicing the word of God that will keep us focused and encouraged on this journey.

We are told that David learned to encourage himself even when his past decisions caused a domino effect in his kingdom. Joseph endured his hard times by not dwelling on the past, but by forgiving. Jacob wrestled with God until God blessed him because his past was coming to confront him. These examples of battling with your past prove that God can still take humans at their worst state and empower them to spread His word. Many of us have testimonies telling how God changed us into the ministers of music we have chosen to be today. It is our testimony of change, not our dwelling inthe past that makes us powerful vessels for the Lord, like those of the Bible.

Pray

Dear Lord, You have not given me the spirit of fear but of power. Sometimes I allow my past to interfere with my present and future life. I pray that I forget those things behind and reach for what is ahead. Help me today to only see my future, so I'll work hard in the present, and not live in my past.

Write

How will I prevent my past from controlling my future? What do I say when the devil continuously reminds me of my past? How do I create goals when my past may be living with me, or near me?

3

Purity of Heart

Psalms 24:4-5, NIV

The one who has clean hands and a pure heart, who does not trust in an idol or swear by a false god. They will receive blessing from the LORD and vindication from God his Savior.

What does cleaning out our hearts entail? The reference text given today speaks about rendering ourselves to God so that we may know right from wrong. Once again it needs to be repeated; our relationship with God will elevate us to a place of wanting to choose right and not feel bad about it. This desire to choose right, exemplifies a purity of heart that promotes a yearning to let others know about God. It is out of that yearning that true music ministry is born. Our ministry gets its breath from us living our lives for His utmost, even if it means letting go of something or someone we love.

The definition of "pure" is uncontaminated. One meaning of the word "heart" is moral feeling. In order to achieve uncontaminated moral feelings we must be washed with the blood of Jesus! We claim the power of the blood in our lives, but do we really understand its significance? "What can wash away my sins, nothing but the blood of Jesus..." is a song we learned as children. Today, this song still shows that the blood of Christ figuratively washes or restores God's children. It is not just about accepting God as Lord; it is a strong bond, a bond of blood that makes this happen. We can, and must achieve uncontaminated moral feelings through Christ's mercy and love. Look, if Moses can go to the mountain, see God, live, and be changed, so can we.

Pray

Dear Lord, I want to thank You for the grace and mercy You have bestowed upon me. May my hands be clean and my heart pure so that I will not lift up idols or swear what is false. Renew me. I pray that everything I do and say may be another step closer to achieving purity of heart.

Write

What is purity of heart to you? Have you achieved it? What do you need to do to accomplish it?

4

I Must Decrease…

John 3:30, NIV

He must become greater; I must become less.

Let's look at the story from the reference text. Some of John's followers started arguing about who should baptize who. Could you imagine? The Son of God is visible on earth and people are arguing about who is going to do what. This is a serious problem. When people argue, it is mostly because they need to prove they are right. Here is where the I's come in. By arguing, they missed God! John had to re-emphasize who he was and what he came to do. So often, in our ministries, we get caught up in the politics of various matters and forget the very purpose of ministry. When there are too many I's, this can cause chaos, confusion, and an atmosphere not fit for ministry growth.

When we decrease, it sets us up for something great. Dominique Maturin, an acquaintance of mine, told me a story. A young girl on the verge of committing suicide came to hear Dominique sing. The experience changed her mind and kept her from committing that act. Suppose Dominique went to each ministry opportunity focused on merely performing and exhibiting her vocal ability. What if Dominique believed it was truly all about her? She could have missed her opportunity to be the vessel God needed to use at that time. When we have moments of ministry we need to come asking God to do one thing, remove self and replace it with all that is Him. We never know who is in the audience when we go to minister. Be prepared in mind, spirit, and song to be a vessel. I must decrease so God can increase!

Pray

Father, You have given me the tools to have an effective ministry. I pray that I don't focus on being right in an argument, being the center of attention, and that I don't dwell on my problems. I pray all of this so that I can be a willing vessel for You. Help me to be a light for those around me for You. I pray, as I grow in You, that others will be drawn to You by how I live my life daily. Additionally, I pray that souls will be drawn to You each time You use me to minister in Your name and for Your glory.

Write

What can I implement to remind myself to decrease so that God is increasingly manifested in me? How can I make sure I don't miss an opportunity to minister because I'm focusing on self?

PART 2

The Fruits We Must Have

But the fruit of the Spirit is love, joy, peace, patience, kindness, goodness, faithfulness, gentleness and self-control. Against such things there is no law.
Galatians 5:22-23, NIV

As we are traveling we will need proper nourishment that we might produce the right kind of fruit. This fruit will enable us to endure, maintain focus, and gain mental clarity.

5

Love

Mark 12:30, NIV

Love the Lord your God with all your heart and with all your soul and with all your mind and with all your strength.

When you hear the word love, what comes to your mind? Love and music ministry are a team. There are three different aspects to explore regarding this partnership. Mark 12:30, deals with loving the Lord with our entire existence. When two human beings fall in love they dedicate time, thoughts, and other emotions to each other. When we fall in love with God, is it any different? The answer is yes, it is better. God's love not only puts a smile on our faces, but transforms us into better people. We often talk about Moses and how his face changed after seeing God. That is just the beginning of what it is like when we possess the love of God. The love that is inside us compels us to share it with others.

This is the good part. As ministers of music we get to share not only the story of Jesus, but the testimony of God's love toward us through the medium of song. We have the glorious opportunity to set to music the hope that Romans 5:5 speaks of, a hope that is real and never fails. It is a hope that is not predicated on getting things, but is based on the fact that God is truthful and always has our best interest in mind. What is hope? It is faith in action. Romans 8:35, paints a picture of loyalty and love. When loyalty is present and strong nothing can tear us from that love.

Let's tie it all together now. When we decided to be a part of the music ministry, it came from a place of love. When we take the time to learn new music, the dedication to perfect its presentation comes from love. The continuous sacrifice of rearranging our schedules for ministry opportunities and rehearsals comes from a place of love. Putting love into action is something we do every time we sing, rehearse, or minister.

Pray

Father, today I want to take the time just to say thank You. Your demonstration of love for me began when You created this world and then again when You gave Your Son. I pray that the love I feel for You will be seen, shown, and felt when I minister. I pray that the love I have for You is strong, true, and powerful.

Write

Do I truly love the Lord with all my heart, mind, and soul? Can others see the love of God through my ministry?

6

Peace

Psalms 34:14, NIV

Turn from evil and do good; seek peace and pursue it.

As Christians we have the Bible, which shows us how to live peacefully. So why is it so hard to choose to be peaceful? In order to be something, you must obtain knowledge and then train yourself to have this quality continuously. Jesus was the most peaceful person the world has ever known. If you look at all the events that happened before His birth and during His mother's pregnancy, He had examples on which to pattern Himself. His parents learned to be at peace with the many obstacles they endured during that time, and those that were to come. When you think of peace, words such as tranquil and serene come to mind. There are many obstacles that come into our lives. Can you be peaceful when they come to you? I heard a friend describe being peaceful in relation to his job. The friend said, "As a Critical Care Nurse I become more calm or peaceful the more critical a patient becomes." We have a responsibility to teach and show peace to those to whom we speak and minister to. We must speak peace to our problems, trials, mountains, giants, and obstacles so that those who encounter our ministry will encounter peace as well.

Pray

Father, I choose so many times to fight battles instead of choosing to be at peace. I pray that I seek peace and pursue it. I pray that as Your Son came to earth and was the epitome of peace, I will follow His example.

Write

How can you exemplify what peace is? What can you say to someone who is going through a trial and needs peace?

7

Patience

Colossians 1:10-12, NIV

So that you may live a life worthy of the Lord and please him in every way: bearing fruit in every good work, growing in the knowledge of God, being strengthened with all power according to his glorious might so that you may have great endurance and patience, and giving joyful thanks to the Father, who has qualified you to share in the inheritance of his holy people in the kingdom of light.

The growth and development of a plant is a very wonderful but tedious process that requires a great deal of effort on the part of the planter. The planter must be sure the plant gets watered, has sufficient sunlight, and is placed in the right soil. Think of your dreams as the plant. Your water would represent the nourishment you need to foster your dream; the sunlight represents the proper arena for your dream to grow and be displayed; and the soil represents the right foundation so that the dream can grow strong. But the process of planting, implementing, and seeing the dream reach its full potential can be filled with so many distractions that you may feel tempted to just give up.

Webster's dictionary defines patience as bearing pain or trials without complaint. Wow!!! How many times have you been faced with a trial but didn't complain. Patience can also be defined as endurance in action. "Patience is a virtue" is an old cliché, but a true adage. It is a quality we should be eager to obtain. Consider how many times you have gotten frustrated trying to learn a new song only to realize later that the greatest part of your frustration emanated from your lack of patience. When you slowed down, isolated the parts, and analyzed how they worked together to form a cohesive whole, it all made sense. That is how we should approach every trial. Unfortunately, we practice patience selectively. I have a challenge for you, for the next 24 hours, choose to have patience. Whether you are in traffic, dealing with a co-worker, waiting for something that you want, or trying to learn something new, remind yourself to be patient.

Patience is the quality that does not surrender to circumstances or succumb under trial; it is the opposite of despondency and is associated with hope.[2]

Pray

Dear Lord, I pray this in order that I may live a life worthy of pleasing You in every way. Cause me to bear fruit in every good work, to grow in the knowledge of God, and to be strengthened with all power according to Your glorious might. Bless me that I may have great endurance, patience, and joyfully give thanks to the Father, who has qualified me to share in the inheritance of the saints in the Kingdom of Light. I pray that I am patient in my present as You prepare me for all You have in store for me in my future.

Write

Write about a time when you put patience into action, what did you learn? Can those in your ministry currently see this quality in you? Do you need to display more patience in an area? How can you remind yourself to be patient?

8

Kindness

Esther 2:9, NIV

She pleased him and won his favor. Immediately he provided her with her beauty treatments and special food. He assigned to her seven female attendants selected from the king's palace and moved her and her attendants into the best place in the harem.

We read the story of Esther and marvel at how God took an orphan and made her queen of a nation. Not only was she a queen, she was willingly used as a vessel for God's work. In the beginning of the story, before she was chosen as queen, she had to prepare for all that was to come with the duties of being a queen. There were many others who were being prepared as well. What stood out about her? Was it her beauty? It was her kindness. Because of her kindness, special attention was given to her. Now what if she was mean or didn't care?

As Music Ministry Leaders we have to be careful in our own lives to be kind. As we engage in music ministry we will encounter varying personality types. An inability to be kind to the pleasant as well as the not so pleasant could result in the mishandling of a situation. Unfortunately, mishandled situations take us off track. Instead of focusing on the plan or journey God has for us, the focus is now on how to mend relationships and clear up misunderstandings.

Simply remember, it is always better to respond with kindness. That practice has the ability to propel us into becoming better individuals. Esther's kindness propelled her to the next stage in her journey. As a result of her continued demonstration of kindness she won the heart of the king.

Pray

Dear Lord, being kind to others is one golden rule we were taught as children. I pray that if I have lost this kindness that You help restore it to me. I pray You clean my heart of the impurities that would cause me not to be kind.

Write

What can you do today to demonstrate kindness? If you have experiences that demonstrate how being kind changed things for the better, write them down in your journal.

9

Temperance

2 Peter 1:6, NIV

And to knowledge, self-control; and to self-control, perseverance; and to perseverance, godliness.

The Greek word for temperance is *enkrateia* from the root word *kratos*, which means strength. In the above scripture temperance also means self-control. The various powers bestowed by God to man are capable of being abused. The right use demands the controlling power of the will under the operation of the Spirit of God. In Acts 24:25 the word temperance follows "righteousness". Righteousness represents God's claim. Therefore, temperance, or self-control, is man's appropriate response. [3] God, by His Holy Spirit, has given us power and powerful gifts and abilities so others may be compelled to Him. If we are not careful with this power, it can be abused for evil purposes. What does that mean? For example the divine ability to put at ease those who are distraught and discouraged can be used negatively to control the emotions of others for selfish benefits. As ministers of music we have been given many talents and powers that we are to operate in under the direction and guidance of the Holy Spirit. However, in the end it is our choice how we use them, for purposes of God or the purposes of the devil.

In 2 Peter 1:6, temperance follows "knowledge," suggesting that we are required to put into practice what is learned.[3] Now, it is time to put temperance into action. How in the world do I accomplish this? Remember everything we do is a choice. Therefore, we need to choose to be in control rather than out of control in every situation. Understand that the talents and even characteristics that you have been given were not meant for your purpose, but for the purposes of God. This is why so many times the Bible speaks of submitting to Him. When we give God our lives then self-control or temperance eventually becomes easier.

Pray

Dear Lord, there are so many times I choose to use my talents for selfish gain. Help me to first submit all that I am to You and secondly, to practice self-control in my everyday life.

Write

Understanding that the proper response to God's righteousness is practicing self-control, ask yourself, how can I exhibit more self-control in my daily life?

10

Faith

Lamentations 3:24-26, *NIV*

I say to myself, "The LORD is my portion; therefore I will wait for him." The LORD is good to those whose hope is in him, to the one who seeks him; it is good to wait quietly for the salvation of the LORD.

Lamentations 3 shows how Jeremiah cried, but also had hope and demonstrated faith. This should be understood; all that he experienced caused him to be humbled as stated in the verse.

This is a clear indication to us that the terrible experiences we face are there to make us stronger, not to tear us down. Jeremiah was given the heavy responsibility of preaching a message of warning that God would use Babylon, despite its own sin, to judge the people of Judah. He had a long road ahead of him, but he maintained the course because he chose to faithfully attend to the work God charged him with. Yes, he did get weary but he didn't give up. He was disappointed but he didn't give up. No matter what was done to him, from the book of Jeremiah to Lamentations, he didn't give up; instead, he remained faithful to his calling from God.

In our ministry, we will take a difficult but rewarding journey. There are going to be times when the spirits and principalities that are not of this world will cause chaos in the ministry as well as individual heartache. Your spirit may even feel cast down by the chaos they cause. But be encouraged by the example set by Jeremiah and maintain the course, finish the work. No matter what may happen or what is said we must have a focused mind and be determined to continue the work God has set in front of us.

My Auntie Bonnye frequently says "If we could only see the end from the beginning we would choose God's way every time."

Pray

Dear Lord, like the many prophets in the Bible who have demonstrated faith while answering Your call, I too want to be faithful to the calling You have for me. In every aspect, I pray that You prepare me for my calling and help to put faith into action.

Write

Are you prepared or strong enough to endure what it takes to continue the ministry? If the answer is no, what must you do to prepare yourself? If the answer is yes, write down why. How do you plan to maintain your strength?

11

Gentleness

2 Timothy 2:24, *NIV*

And the Lord's servant must not be quarrelsome
but must be kind to everyone, able to teach, not resentful.

This text speaks of exhibiting gentleness in teaching others. As ministers of music we have the responsibility to teach utilizing both what we say, and what we sing. However, that teaching begins in us as leaders. We have to take the time, not only to learn the lyrics, but to also understand the meaning behind the words. When we truly understand a song's meaning someone in the audience can say God sent me here to hear that song. In our ministry there are many people who will come to us after we sing. They may say something nice, or they may be mean. Regardless of what comes out of them, it is our responsibility to demonstrate gentleness, be kind, and point them to Christ.

Music Ministry can be difficult at times because we do not know who is coming, nor do we know the reasons they have come. Despite their varying reasons for attending, God uses our meekness and gentleness as an opportunity to show Himself strong. Therefore, when faced with unkind temperaments we should choose to say, "God bless you", over giving someone a piece of our minds. Gentleness can be confusing to a person who has every intention of being negative. It is in that moment that God can use us as vessels to point others to Him.

Pray

Dear Lord, we live in a world that demonstrates cruelty on every level. With all that You have taught me, I ask that I show gentleness to my fellow man. I pray that I'll be gentle in my ministry, apt to teach, and patient as I instruct others. I also pray to be used as a vessel bearing Your truth and leading all to repentance.

Write

Where in your life and or music ministry can you be gentle?

12

Longsuffering

I Timothy 1:16, NIV

But for that very reason I was shown mercy so that in me, the worst of sinners, Christ Jesus might display his immense patience as an example for those who would believe in him and receive eternal life.

Longsuffering is that quality of self-restraint in the face of provocation which does not hastily retaliate or promptly punish; it is the opposite of anger, and is associated with mercy.[4] One example of longsuffering many can identify with would be a person going through cancer. If you think about it, from the time the individual is diagnosed they have already gone through many emotions. Then add the emotional process of deciding to have surgery or therapy for removal. And the question of, what if it doesn't work? If it does work, there is another set of emotions associated with remission. Those who have, and even those who know someone who has battled cancer know that any kind of stress can work against treatment making it imperative to not only learn to heal the body, but the mind as well. Here is where longsuffering is put into action.

The journey is long with physical, mental, and emotional suffering. We do understand that not everyone wins by going into remission, but they win when they continuously allow God to keep them. In those moments they prove it is possible to have faith in the midst of suffering.

How long did you have to run your music department without support or proper resources? How many times have you started rehearsal with just the faithful few? How many times have your musicians not shown up for rehearsals or ministry outings? But for that reason I show mercy...I Timothy 1:16.

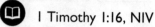

Pray

Father, I pray that my heart, mind, and soul continually strive for the perfection You exemplified while on earth. Let not my endurance be overcome with weakness, but cause me to lean on You during my longsuffering and have faith that You will keep me from falling.

Write

How can I have the strength to endure longsuffering?

13

Joy

Psalms 126:5-6, NIV

Those who sow with tears will reap with songs of joy. Those who go out weeping, carrying seed to sow, will return with songs of joy, carrying sheaves with them.

The day I found out about my "Big Sister" passing I was terribly upset. It was Christmas time and here I was getting ready to travel to Georgia for my sister's funeral. During the time before her passing, just hearing that she wasn't feeling well really bothered me. If you knew DW, she had an infectious personality that would cause anyone to smile. Just the thought of her not being able to spread the joy she was known for sharing disheartened me. Hearing of her passing, I was ready to be distraught, but God had different plans for me. God decided that He was not going to let me be emotional for very long.

The day I was traveling to Georgia, I received a phone call from a dear friend. She made me understand that God wanted me to use one of the talents my sister saw in me for someone else. There was no time to wallow; I had to be available for God's use. But the story didn't stop there. We all understand that grieving is a process you go through. Well, a few days later, another friend called and was wondering if she made the right choice about stepping out on faith. The Lord gave me scripture and words of encouragement. One of the statements I made to her was, "there are certain blessings that only come when you praise God; when you show joy." These were the precise words I needed to press past my own moment of heaviness.

Sometimes when we are at what could possibly be our worst state; God finds joy for us. During my time of encouraging others I found joy in God. Now that's amazing!

Pray

Father, Your word states that they that sow in tears shall reap in joy. I pray that when I bring tears to You I see the joy You have waiting for me. Let me always know the joy I have in You. Knowing that You love me and will never leave me is priceless.

Write

How can you turn a time of tears into a time of joy in your ministry?

14

Made to Be...

Genesis 50:20-21, ESV

As for you, you meant evil against me, but God meant it for good,
to bring it about that many people should be kept alive, as they are today.
So do not fear; I will provide for you and your little ones."
Thus he comforted them and spoke kindly to them. ESV

The music industry can be cruel and filled with many that have selfish motives. There will be times in music ministry when people say they have come to help, but are really there to destroy. That sounds horrible doesn't it? Matthew 10:16 states, "Be wise as a serpent and harmless as a dove." Galatians 6:7 states "Be ye not deceived." These words were given as sound counsel, but forgotten when the time came to recall or use that counsel. It simply wasn't used. In the music industry you must learn to see with spiritual eyes. So you can decipher between what God is allowing for the growth of the ministry and what the devil has devised for the destruction of ministry. In either scenario, remember that people are merely instruments. Therefore, as the music ministry leaders you must be ready and willing to forgive immediately. You have heard it many times: pray without ceasing. This is a must.

- Joseph's life is a great example of some of the obstacles you will go through in this Music industry.
- Joseph was taught and trained for many years: he was setup. Can you remember or track how you were setup in ministry?
- Joseph's brothers saw him as a threat. Have you ever felt uneasy following your training in God for ministry? Have you found yourself asking why others seem to be against you or even seem to hate you?
- Joseph's brothers sold him into slavery. In what ways do friends, family, job,

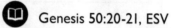

home life, or other environmental circumstances seem to imprison you?

- Potiphar's wife accused Joseph falsely. Have you ever been falsely accused?
- Joseph must have cried and wondered where God was in this process. Have you ever been in the place where you feel like everything is wrong and began to wonder where God was? Did you ask God, why me?
- Joseph was made governor and helped save Egypt from famine. Where has God placed you? Can you see what He is setting you up for?

Note the life of Joseph. Difficulty will come, but the difference between success and failure is how you endure difficulty. Put a plan for faith and endurance into action. "I am made to be______________________." (Fill in the blank.)

Pray

Lord, please allow me to wear the fruit of the spirit as literally as I would wear clothes. Help me to understand that the harshness of man doesn't mean defeat for me. Instead, help me to automatically respond with forgiveness and wisdom.

Write

In the face of difficulty are you staying faithful to your ministry or have you become bitter? How do you plan to stay focused and not become disdained by the journey ahead?

PART 3

The Purpose Of Ministry

We have come to the part of the journey where difficult questions often arise. What is my purpose? Have I kept God as my GPS (navigator), or am I choosing my own direction? The answers to these questions lets us know if we are on the right path or if we need to go in a new direction.

15

Music

Lamentations 3:63, KJV

Behold their sitting down, and their rising up; I am their music.

Music gets its definition from the Greek word for symphonic, which means a sounding together. Another definition found in the Wikipedia Internet Dictionary states that it is the combination of sound and silence. Neither of these definitions speaks of the effects of music. In today's society, we have heard about so many instances where people have committed some crime or act of violence, including murder and suicide, as a result of music. We see young people participating in inappropriate behavior as a result of the music to which they are exposed.

Music can also have very positive effects. When you read the text above, it indicates that no matter what mental state or circumstance we are in, God is our music. We can be reminded that David used his harp to calm the evil spirits that were bothering Saul. David used the service of song as a regular part of religious worship. Further, he composed psalms for the priests and the congregation as they journeyed to the annual feasts of that day. The influence resulted in freeing the nation from idolatry. Music, when it's used correctly, can release the Holy Spirit to penetrate hearts, renew souls, and transform lives. It is our responsibility to ask God to use us as instruments of praise as we minister to others with our music.[5]

Pray

Father, You are my music. I pray You will use music in my life to be a source of ministry to others and for my personal spiritual development. Lord in my sitting down and my rising up You are my music.

Write

What does music mean to you? Do you think you need to monitor your selection of music? How can music be your source of ministry?

16

Ministry Or Money

Matthew 9:9, *NIV*

As Jesus went on from there, he saw a man named Matthew sitting at the tax collector's booth. "Follow me," he told him, and Matthew got up and followed him.

What is more important, your venue or the hundreds of people who will hear your ministry? Are you preparing for ministry or to perform? There are many debates that could come from the previous questions, but here is the reality about ministry: It begins with our personal relationship with God. That relationship constrains us. It is how we know our focus needs to be placed solely on ministry. To remain focused there are a few questions we should ask ourselves. What do I want, ministry or fame? Am I putting God first in all my decisions? During my childhood, I was exposed to the secular music profession. I witnessed secular artists commit many hours to being in the studio; I listened and learned, through the discussions that occurred, what it took to be successful secularly. As an adult I was involved in the Christian side of professional music. Every choir or group I have worked with has had to face and answer the question of motivation: Ministry/Money? Please note both are possible to have. Your driving force should not be the focus on money, to get rich. The focus should be where does God want to take the ministry. Trust Him in that and I guarantee He will provide while your heart is pure in service to Him.

The rich-young-ruler wanted to know how to get into the kingdom of heaven and Jesus told him to give away all that he owned. The rich-young-ruler went away because he was not willing to give up all he had. When Jesus met Matthew He told Matthew to come follow Him and he did. Matthew walked away from position and money for ministry.

Pray

Dear Lord, You have given me a ministry, help me to embrace the work You have laid out for me. Today as I pray for all the needs of ministry, I lay them at Your feet. I ask that I not worry about my personal needs, but focus on the journey of the ministry.

Write

I want to leave a few scriptures with you and then you decide what will win your devotion: Ministry/Money?

I Chronicles 6:32	*Ephesians 5:19*
I Chronicles 23:5	*I Peter 5:2*
Ecclesiastes 5:10	*Leviticus 19:13*
Ecclesiastes 7:10	*Romans 4:4*
Psalms 9:1	*I Samuel 2:35*
Psalms 57:7	*Matthew 7:7*

17

Grace

I Timothy 1:14, *NIV*

The grace of our Lord was poured out on me abundantly, along with the faith and love that are in Christ Jesus.

If not for Your grace where would I be? To be in any ministry is an honor. But the gift of music ministry has so many responsibilities. What is grace? *Grace is enabling power sufficient for progression. Grace divine is an indispensable gift from God for development, improvement, and character expansion. Without God's grace there are certain limitations, weaknesses, flaws, impurities, and faults (i.e. carnality) humankind cannot overcome. Therefore, it is necessary to increase in God's grace for added perfection, completeness, and flawlessness. If there were an example of grace in music ministry, it would have been David. David not only used grace to rule a kingdom, he used the grace bestowed upon him to write music. The songs that he wrote in Psalms are still used today to encourage, uplift, and praise.

Reflecting on our personal testimonies should energize us to continue in ministry for years and not feel tired. Think about the people we minister to; what are they looking for? Can we share our story of grace through our ministry?

Pray

What does grace mean to you?

Write

Dear Lord, grace is a gift like so many You have given to us. Help me to appreciate this gift and share it with others. When my ministry has to reach out to those who have yet to understand grace, please impart Your Holy Spirit and make me a vessel that extends grace to all who encounter my ministry.

18

Shew Thyself

Ephesians 4:11-13, *NIV*

So Christ himself gave the apostles, the prophets, the evangelists, the pastors and teachers, to equip his people for works of service, so that the body of Christ may be built up until we all reach unity in the faith and in the knowledge of the Son of God and become mature, attaining to the whole measure of the fullness of Christ.

Do you have a gift? The answer is yes. The next question is what is it? There is a saying that says: "My natural abilities are God's suggestions for my life's work." When I searched for my gifts, I second-guessed every gift I had. I have been singing since I was a little girl. Although I love it, I wasn't sure it was a gift God wanted me to use for Him professionally. God placed me in certain situations and places so that I could test the gifts He gave me. Instead of trying to guess what they were, I went through the wilderness experience. When you go into the wilderness it is just you and God. It is a transformation journey for you to be ready to do God's work. While on this path, I made one crucial request of God, "God, shew thyself; help me to understand what you want me to do."

As I continued studying and praying for the clarity of my ministry, I started seeking those who had a love relationship with God and who also loved to use their talents for Him. So God surrounded me with Pillars (the people God places in your life to uphold you, encourage you, pray over you, and speak the word of God into your life). Every sermon I heard was one for strength and rehabilitation. Every place I went, God used the occasion to show me what I must do. When I was strong enough, the Pillars God used were no longer there. God used Pillars, places, sermons, and people to show me my gifts.

In the past, my music ministry encompassed both singing and working for various Christian artists. Today, when God calls I minister through song. Thank God for showing me my gifts. My youngest daughter frequently asks, "Mommy, when are you going to sing?" Those words are a blessing to my ears. By the warmth of the Spirit and the words of the Father I know I have followed through on my ministry.

Pray

Father in heaven, You are glorious, marvelous and gracious. Thank You for the gifts You have given me. God I am asking You to "Shew Thyself" to me so that I may have clarity in my ministry and my relationship with You...

Write

What is your gift? Do you really want to know? And how will you use it?

19

Don't Close Without Christ

Luke 14:23, NIV

"Then the master told his servant, 'Go out to the roads and country lanes and make them come in, so that my house will be full.'"

It is essential that the music ministry remember that music is ministry. I attended many "Christian" concerts that were purely entertainment. The Christian artists forgot about what they were doing and the purpose of it. Ministry. If we are doing a concert or program there must be an invitation to Christ. Isn't the main point to bring others to Christ? To preach, or in this case sing or play, the Word for others to be compelled to seek a life with Christ?

A few years ago I was singing in a duo. For weeks as we prepared for an upcoming program, we prayed for those who would be in attendance. When we arrived we were greeted with such warmth and love that we knew it was a God-given assignment. I remember being very nervous, more than usual, about the outcome of this program. I kept praying leading up to and throughout our set. As the program progressed the Spirit of God was filling the hearts and minds of the audience. It was our plan to close with prayer, but being obedient to the Holy Spirit, we called for the prayer warriors in the audience to come to the front. Then it happened! Almost the entire audience lined up in front of the prayer warriors and we prayed for all of them. What a moment of ministry!

We were so overcome with joy that to this day, we look back on it with boisterous praise. Never close your program without Him, you don't know who is there waiting to come to Christ.

Pray

Father never let me close a moment of ministry without You. I must be invisible and You visible so they will be drawn to You. Your Spirit must fill their hearts through the ministry You have placed in me.

Write

What plan do you have for the invitation to Christ at your next moment of ministry?

PART 4

Commitment To Ministry

Here is where we implement what we have learned on our journey. We have learned many things over these past few weeks. It is time to put it into practice. But before we do, ask yourself if you are ready. Are you ready to commit? Are you really ready for all ministry gives…and takes?

As my friend Timothy Anderson would say "I am going in…"

20

Commitment

Job 5:8, *KJV*

But if it were I, I would appeal to God; I would lay my cause before him.

Years ago, I was hired to work for an acappella singing group. We flew to Chattanooga, TN, and then headed to Huntsville, AL to minister. On the way, we stopped at Shoney's Restaurant. When we arrived, breakfast was ending in five minutes. We asked the waitress to please extend it a little longer for us. The waitress asked her manager and they served breakfast a little longer just for us. I was grateful because I was hungry! After we ate, the group ministered in song for the staff. As we were getting into our van, a gentleman stopped us. We were pressed for time; however, we ministered to the gentleman for just five minutes and exchanged testimonies. As we did, we learned that he was a minister visiting Alabama from California. He described how he thought he was listening to the radio as the group sung in the restaurant. It was only when we left that he realized he was listening to live music.

Pressed for time we left and started down the highway. One of the members of the group said, "look up ahead, a tornado is crossing the highway." When we drove up to the after effects of the tornado, there was an 18 wheeler turned on its side, a house with extensive damage (you could see straight into the house from the highway), cars with windows shattered, and trees cut in half. Just 5 minutes and a commitment to God saved us. What if we didn't stop to minister with that gentleman? What if we just ignored all the others to whom we ministered? God is awesome. Praise the Lord!

When you are committed to ministry you learn to be obedient to the promptings of the Holy Spirit. You hear His voice or sometimes He performs an action and you know it is God speaking.

Pray

Dear Jesus, thank You for all the things You protect me from that enable me to continue ministering for You. I ask that You continue speaking to me and through me. I will study and spend time with You so that I will know when You are speaking. My commitment to You is to be true in every way.

Write

What testimony do you have where you can say God saved you? Do you know when God is speaking to you and if so, how? Does this testimony reinforce your commitment?

21

Unity

Psalms 133:1, NIV

How good and pleasant it is when God's people live together in unity!

Webster's dictionary defines unity as the quality or state of not being multiple; a condition of harmony; continuity without deviation or change (as in purpose or action); the quality or state of being made one; a combination or ordering of parts in a literary or artistic production that constitutes a whole or promotes an undivided total effect. In any ministry there must be unity of purpose and spirit. To have one goal, one mission, and one spirit is a big part of a successful music ministry. This doesn't mean there will not be disagreements or arguments.

Unity, I have learned, is seen in those who go through trials successfully and now minister in harmony. Unity is a strength that comes from working together, praying through trials together, and staying together no matter what. Unity is being able to have a disagreement now but have fun later. Unity is smiling in your ministry and giving a word of love even when discouraged or disappointed. Unity is standing tall in public and in private. Unity is fellowship outside of worship. Unity is knowing we need to pray when no one has said a word. Unity is our ministry as a united front against the devil.

Pray

Father in heaven, many times we are not unified in ministry because there is something we need to fix in us. Today, I ask that you help me to see and change anything in me that causes my ministry not be unified. How good and pleasant it is when brothers live together in unity. Let my ministry be unified in spirit, purpose, mission, and direction.

Write

If there is no unity in my ministry, what can I do to make it unified? Is there anything I am doing, or not doing, to contribute to the group not being unified?

22

Fasting

Matthew 6:16-18, NIV

When you fast, do not look somber as the hypocrites do, for they disfigure their faces to show men they are fasting. I tell you the truth; they have received their reward in full. But when you fast, put oil on your head and wash your face, so that it will not be obvious to men that you are fasting, but only to your Father, who is unseen; and your Father, who sees what is done in secret, will reward you.

When do you fast? Do you have to fast? I have learned there are some things that only come by prayer and fasting. To overcome obstacles or to have a deep desire fulfilled are the two main reasons for fasting. According to David A. Strands, "The truth is many people in the Bible fasted. Moses fasted on Mount Sinai in Exodus 34:28. According to I Samuel 1:7 Hannah fasted when she wanted a son from God. David fasted on several occasions. Many more examples of fasting are found in the Old Testament. But fasting is not just an Old Testament practice. Jesus fasted in the wilderness, (Matthew 4). John the Baptist taught his disciples to fast, (Mark 2:18, Luke 5:33). Some found fault with Jesus' disciples for their failure to fast often, (Matthew 9:14, 15). Cornelius fasted before his Caesarean vision, (Acts 10:30). The church at Antioch fasted when they sent Paul and Barnabas on their first missionary journey (Acts 13:3)."[6]

Fasting should be an important part of a Christian's life. Although we are never commanded to fast, "per se," it is very important for Christians to fast. I believe it is scriptural for Christians to fast; it is an act of faith. When we fast, we deprive ourselves of the fulfillment of our wants and in so doing, we help build up our ability to overcome sinful desires of the flesh. I think we should understand that fasting should be seen by God and not man (Matthew 6:16-18). Jesus was not condemning fasting, he was condemning those who were boasting of their fasting. Obviously, such is hypocrisy and would not be honorable to God.

Overcoming obstacles can be traced back to overcoming self. In order to overcome self you should submit yourself to God and develop a relationship with Him for growth. But as we all know, the flesh is a hard thing to overcome. Fasting is giving up something in your life in order to overcome obstacles. It is a sacrifice that makes you soar upward and forward. In my ministry, fasting is a must.

Pray

Father, how wonderful You are! God, at this time I have strong desires for my ministry. Please show me how You can fulfill these desires. Teach me what I must do to fulfill them. When I fast let it be unto You and not for show. Let me learn to fast for the needs of the ministry.

Write

Strong desires for ministry require willing sacrifice and great planning, what are you willing to do to fulfill those desires?

23

The Base of My Ministry

Colossians 4:2, NIV

Devote yourselves to prayer, being watchful and thankful.

Pastor Laurent S. Governor stated in a sermon "The base of your ministry must be prayer." In order for us to reflect the very values of the heart of God we must be a people who know how to pray. "Prayer is the most intense of our spiritual discipline," states Pastor Laurent S. Governor.

Why is this important? It gives our ministry power and direction. There are many examples we can give, but let us focus on a few:

- Abraham prayed and Lot was delivered.
- Esther prayed and received clarity on how to save her people.
- Naomi prayed for Ruth and she was blessed with a wonderful husband.
- David prayed and won many battles. Through prayer God granted him war strategies.
- Solomon prayed for wisdom to rule a nation and be true to his father's legacy.

We must have a persistent prayer life in our ministries. It is this constant contact that allows the Spirit to bring truth to us and in us. Prayer is what replaces guessing, with clear and precise direction. Prayer is the answer.

Pray

God the ministry You have placed in my hands is one I am dedicating to You. Like Solomon asked You for wisdom, I am asking You to teach me to fervently pray. I don't want to come to You with a fake voice, an uneasy heart, and a list of wants. I want to come before You with the heart of the ministry and a request for understanding.

Write

Where have you placed prayer on your list of priorities? How can your ministry become a ministry based in prayer?

24

Leadership

Peter 5:2, *NIRV*

"Be shepherds of God's flock, the believers who are under your care. Serve as their leaders. Don't serve them because you have to. Instead, do it because you want to. That's what God wants you to do. Don't do it because you want to get more and more money. Do it because you really want to serve."

As leaders in music ministry, we must be armored, ready, and anchored in Christ. If you are in leadership or getting ready for it, be committed to prayer, fasting, reading the word of God, studying the word of God, practicing the word of God, and praying some more.

Leading can be quite challenging. It requires good decision-making skills, strong delegation, and understanding of the role of a servant-leader. However, with the challenges come great rewards. In music ministry, those rewards are more powerful when centered in Christ. There is a statement I have come to reflect on before every moment of ministry, whether I am singing or preaching.

"I purpose myself today to be open to the Holy Spirit, so that I can be used as a vessel to glorify God and edify man."

Please note, if you have not taken the time to study, to have a committed prayer life, to routinely improve on your skills and gifts God cannot pull it out of you during moments of ministry. Take the tools that you have been given from this book, other resources that God has provided for you, your training, and the word of God to let Him use you to set the atmosphere. I urge you, please do not take your leadership for granted. What you do or do not do can depend on a soul choosing Jesus. We are not perfect at all, that's where Jesus comes in and reminds us, we are made to worship and setup to serve.

Pray

God, I come to You today unworthy of Your grace and gifts of love. I ask for discernment to protect the ministry You have given me. Lord, cause me to lead with love.

Write

What kind of leader are you? What kind of leader does your team think you are? Are the answers to those questions in line with what God wants? Whatever your answers are to these questions, what plans have you put in place to implement the leader that God wants you to become?

PRAYER FOR THE MUSIC MINISTER

My Seven Days of Prayer

Prayer is personal and one of the ways to communicate with God. During the next seven days, try taking your relationship with God to the next level. Every day, seek to learn and grow. You can use the format presented in this book or choose your own. Your topics can be things that have been at the heart of your ministry or a topic you have wanted God to reveal to you. Make this time the start of more great times with God. Make sure you journal throughout this time what God is revealing to you. Take your ministry to the next level by making your relationship with God number one.

The Prayer of a Music Minister

For the Prayer you will need to read the following texts to understand and know what you are praying for.

- *I Peter 5:8*
- *Matthew 16*
- *Isaiah 40:11*
- *Acts 12*
- *Philippians 4:6 & 7*
- *Psalms 22:3*
- *Job 1*
- *Matthew 5:13:16*
- *Ephesians 2*

You can add to this prayer per the needs of your music ministry.

The Prayer

Lord, I come to You placing the ministry You have allowed me to have in Your hands. There are many things I am unsure of, so for this I come to You. Open my eyes to recognize the potential of the demonic in all areas of this ministry. Teach me to war against their potential in prayer and in the application of wisdom. Teach me how to be patient and wait on You. Help me in all areas of my life and ministry to release the power of prayer and praise. Finally, may I always use my influence to compel others to seek You and bless Your name. Amen.

Write

Over the next 7 days, continue to write your prayers. Begin here and feel free to continue in a new notebook or device.

The End of the Beginning

I want to take this time to say thank you for taking this journey with me. Welcome Levites, to the next level in your ministry and your walk. If you have honestly and actively journeyed through this book, then I hope it is apart of the agitation that fosters positive change and points you to a deeper relationship with God.

I am praying for you. The road traveled by a Christian is filled with great moments of praise and obstacles of faith. The road for a Levite ministry member is filled with great moments of praise, difficult obstacles of faith, a responsibility to be a positive servant-leader, routine of improving skills/gifts, and a devoted personal worship life. The road traveled by a Levite leader is filled with great moments of praise, difficult obstacles of faith, a responsibility to be a great positive servant, a devoted personal worship life, routine of improving skills/gifts, and a commitment to dive so deep into the word of God that you look like Moses after seeing God on the mountain. This is the Levite life!

I look forward to hearing your testimonies. Let us continue to press toward the mark, introducing Christ and transforming lives with God as our leader.

Continue the journey to which you are called one step at a time, one prayer at a time, and change one life at a time.

Sincerely,
Levite Richards

RESOURCES

1. White, Ellen G. Patriarchs and Prophets, Mountain View, California: Pacific Press Publishing Association p.594
2. Vine, WMerrill F. Unger, Merrill F. Unger Vine's Complete Expository Dictionary, p. 377
3. Vine's Complete Expository Dictionary, p.620.
4. Vine's Complete Expository Dictionary, p 377
5. White, Ellen G. Patriarchs and Prophets, Mountain View, California: Pacific Press Publishing Association p.711
6. Stand, David A. "SHOULD A CHRISTIAN FAST?" January 1, 1986. Web. Nov 2009. www.newtestamentchurch.org/.

WELCOME TO THE NATSEL FAMILY

You have just finished reading one of the products from our Natsel Family. Please note, we are here to help you "Live a Positively Mpowered Life." We look forward to seeing you soon, shopping at our store, at one of our events, online sessions, at a leadership seminar, or reading another one of our books.

Natsel
Plan Your Work and Work Your Plan
www.natsel.org

Zamar
Made to Worship Setup to Serve
www.zamarnatsel.com

MpoweredMe
Right tools, Right Mindset
www.Mpoweredme.net

CPSIA information can be obtained
at www.ICGtesting.com
Printed in the USA
FSHW021402251020

9 781948 877497